GENEROUS ANGER
The Story of George Orwell

GENEROUS ANGER
The Story of George Orwell

William J. Boerst

620 South Elm Street, Suite 223
Greensboro, North Carolina   27406
http://www.morganreynolds.com

GENEROUS ANGER: THE STORY OF GEORGE ORWELL

Library of Congress Cataloging-in-Publication Data

Boerst, William J.
  Generous anger: the story of George Orwell / William J. Boerst.
    p. cm.
  Includes bibliographical references (p.) and index.
  ISBN 1-883846-74-9 (lib. bdg.)
    1. Orwell, George, 1903-1950--Juvenile literature. 2. Authors, English--20th
century--Biography--Juvenile literature. [1. Orwell, George, 1903-1950. 2. Authors,
English.] I. Title.

  PR6029.R8 Z5877 2001
  828'.91209--dc21
  [B]

2001030877

Printed in the United States of America
First Edition

To Nancy,
who nurtures writing in others

Contents

Eric Arthur Blair was also known as the writer George Orwell.
(Courtesy of University College London.)

Chapter One

Childhood Pain and Joy

Like most middle-class British boys his age, eight-year-old Eric Blair (who would later change his name to George Orwell) moved away from home to attend boarding school. This was a difficult change. Eric began wetting his bed, a habit he had outgrown about four years earlier. The school treated these accidents as if Eric were wetting his bed deliberately. One day the headmistress, Mrs. Wilkes, called Eric into a room where she was having tea with another woman. The other woman was large and wore riding pants. "Here is a little boy," Mrs. Wilkes said to the other woman, "who wets his bed every night." Then she boomed to Eric: "Do you know what I am going to do if you wet your bed again? I am going to get the Sixth Form to beat you."

The other woman acted shocked and responded, "I should think so!" Eric did not realize that the Sixth Form was the older class. Instead, he thought that the woman having tea with Mrs. Wilkes was "Mrs. Form." He felt ashamed to have another person know about his problem.

Not too long after that incident, Eric wet the bed again. This time the dormitory matron ordered, "Report yourself to the headmaster after breakfast!" The headmaster, "a round-shouldered curiously offish-looking man, not large but shambling in gait, with a chubby face which was like that of an overgrown baby," took a riding crop from his cupboard, and while lecturing him soundly, bent Eric over and beat him with the crop. Afterwards, Eric walked out of the office grinning and informed some boys that the beating had not hurt. The headmistress overheard his remark and called him back.

This time the headmaster beat Eric so hard that he broke the riding crop. "Look what you made me do!" he yelled, showing Eric the broken end. Eric began to cry, not so much from pain as from feeling upset that he had wet his bed and now broken the headmaster's crop. He felt lonely and helpless. He felt that, no matter how hard he tried, he could not be good. Eric may have wet his bed only once more after that. Although it seemed the harsh punishment had cured him, Eric often wondered later what those beatings had cost him.

Eric Blair was born in 1903 in Bengal, India, to Richard and Ida Blair. Richard worked for the British government in the Indian

The Blairs in 1916: Eric, Ida, Avril, and Richard.
(Courtesy of University College London.)

Opium Department. India, then a colony of the British Empire, had developed a profitable trade growing poppies and selling opium, a drug produced from poppies, to the Chinese. After Britain took control of the country, they oversaw the opium trade. Eric was Richard and Ida's second child; his sister Marjorie was born in 1898. In 1904 their mother, Ida, took the two children back to England. It was common then for British parents living in India to return their children to England for school. As an overseer in the Indian Opium Department, Richard had seven years remaining in his career. He remained in Bengal alone.

Once back in England, Ida and her two children settled in a market town named Henley-on-Thames. Mrs. Blair called their house Ermadale (for ERic and MArjorie). The countryside was attractive and perfect for raising children. They had plenty of opportunities to climb trees, swim, play with toy soldiers, pick blackberries, and buy candy from the sweet shop.

Eric's first playmates outside the family were the children of a plumber who lived nearby. Eventually, Eric's mother forbade him to play with them, most likely because they were not middle-class children. An older boy, Humphrey Dakin, sometimes let Eric go fishing with him and his friends. Otherwise, Eric passed the days alone or in the company of women. He learned to read early and spent much of his time surrounded by books.

During the summer of 1907, when Eric was four years old, his father came home on leave from India for three months. After he returned for the four years until his retirement, Ida gave birth to their third child and second daughter, Avril, in 1908.

At age five, Eric dictated an original poem to his mother, who recorded it on paper. He later recalled, "I had the lonely child's habit of making up stories and holding conversations with imaginary persons, and I think from the very start my literary ambitions were mixed up with the feeling of being isolated and undervalued."

Because of certain remarks from various women visiting his mother, Eric formed the impression that women saw men as undesirable brutes. He was the only male in the home and therefore thought that his mother disapproved of him. This notion remained even after he learned that he had been his mother's favorite.

By the time he turned eight, Eric had already read *Tom Sawyer*, Ballantine's *Coral Island*, and *Rebecca of Sunnybrook Farm*. The day before his birthday, he sneaked a peek at the present his mother had wrapped for him—a copy of Swift's *Gulliver's Travels*. He could not wait, so he began reading the book that night.

It was customary for middle-class families in Britain to send their children to boarding school. In 1911 eight-year-old Eric was enrolled in St. Cyprian's, a respected preparatory school sixty miles south of London. But the Blairs were struggling and could not afford the school fees. Sometimes, headmasters would reduce tuition fees for promising students in the hope of gaining prestige if that student were later accepted into one of the respected public schools. (In Britain, public schools are the equivalent of private schools in the United States.) Because Eric showed promise, he was admitted at half cost. This privilege, however, worked against him. In an effort to motivate him to perform better, the headmaster told him that his tuition had been reduced. Eleven-year-old Eric felt ashamed at being labeled a charity case.

The curriculum at St. Cyprian's prepared students for entrance exams to public school. They memorized dates, passages from books, and rules of Latin grammar. Eric's classes included languages, history, and mathematics.

Looking back years later, some classmates agreed with Eric's recollection that life at St. Cyprian's had been a cruel experience, but others disagreed. Perhaps the reason for those different views lay in the forceful personality of the headmistress, Mrs. Wilkes. She paid particular attention to her favorites, who often came from the moneyed class. To the others, she showed indifference or hostility. One classmate recalled that Eric greased his hair so that Mrs. Wilkes could not pull it as easily.

There was little privacy at the school. Each dormitory room had three to five beds. Lavatory doors could not be fastened shut. During the night, the matron would walk the dormitory halls in soft slippers, listening for talkers.

The day began at 7:15 when all the boys were herded into the ice cold water of the school's swimming pool. The boys had to swim the length of the pool before drying themselves on damp towels. Next, they met in front of the gym for physical training, and then they went to chapel. Breakfast usually consisted of cold cereal and bread with margarine.

St. Cyprian's was successful in preparing its students for the public schools. However, Eric grew to hate the endless memorization, which was carried out with little concern for actual learning. He was also bothered by the chasm between the rich boys and the middle class boys. Eric's family lived on a few hundred pounds a year, but many boys had fathers who made more than a thousand pounds a year. Often the wealthier boys would cross-examine the others to determine how much money their families had. Eric later reflected: "Perhaps the greatest cruelty one can inflict on a child is to send it to school among children richer than itself. A child conscious of poverty will suffer snobbish agonies such as a grown-up can scarcely imagine."

This disparity in financial standing took many forms. The wealthier boys could afford riding and shooting lessons, toys, and candy. They often spent school holidays in fancy resorts. Meanwhile, Eric would be continually reminded of his place. If he wanted to buy a cricket bat or a model airplane, Mrs. Wilkes would ask, "Do you think that's the sort of thing a boy like you should buy?"

One custom at the school was to give each boy a cake on his birthday, complete with candles. But Mrs. Wilkes decided that Eric's parents could not afford a cake. Each birthday, the young boy suffered the disgrace of not having a cake, which advertised his family's class.

After World War I started in 1914, school authorities constantly reminded the boys about the importance of military training. Returning soldiers visited the campus and told of their experiences. In wartime, Mr. and Mrs. Wilkes' emphasis on character seemed more relevant. The school magazine published tributes to alumni who had lost their lives in the war and praised them as true heroes.

The boys did their part to help in the war effort. They grew vegetables, sent parcels to the front lines, and knitted socks and mufflers for British troops. They also visited the wounded at a nearby convalescent camp. Eric became caught up in war fever. At age eleven he wrote a patriotic poem that his family submitted to their local newspaper. When it was published, even Mrs. Wilkes was impressed.

Eric liked some of the teachers at St. Cyprian's. He admired his Latin teacher, Mr. Knowles, a man with long hair who wore baggy suits. Eric also had fond memories of Mr. Sillar, who taught geography and drawing. He sometimes took the boys butterfly hunting, sharing his passion for natural history with them.

One boy who went butterfly-hunting was Cyril Connolly. He had a somewhat flattened nose and a pronounced forehead. Cyril was Eric's age and came from a middle-class family, too. Their love of books and reading soon made them best friends.

One of their favorite authors was H.G. Wells. When they were lucky enough to get a copy of his *The Country of the Blind*, one kept stealing the book from the other. Years later, Eric recalled, "I can still remember at four o'clock on a midsummer morning, with the school fast asleep and the sun slanting through the window, creeping down a passage to Connolly's dormitory where I knew the book would be beside his bed."

Some of Eric's early writing practice took the form of responding to newspaper advertisements. Eric wrote a letter as a joke to a woman who said she had a solution to being overweight. In her response, she told Eric to visit her in London immediately. Because Eric had

Young Eric enjoyed the writings of H. G. Wells.
(Courtesy of the University of Illinois Library at Urbana-Champaign.)

signed his letter E.A. Blair, she assumed he was a woman and advised, "Do come before ordering your summer frocks, as after taking my course your figure will have altered out of recognition." She continued writing until he tired of the charade, explaining that he had lost weight through another method.

Just as the summer holiday was ending in 1914, Eric met the Buddicoms. Jacintha, age thirteen; her sister, Guiny, age seven; and her brother, Prosper, age ten, were playing cricket when they saw a boy standing on his head. They asked why he was doing this. Eric answered, "You are noticed more if you stand on your head than if you are right way up." From that point on, the children became close friends and saw each other every day. Their family sometimes even took Eric along on vacation. Jacintha and Eric enjoyed discussing books and comparing stories about each other's pets.

The children played games such as hangman and rummy. They also collected stamps, coins, cigarette cards, and birds' eggs. Eric fished and hunted with Prosper . Once, the two boys killed a hedgehog and tried cooking it in clay, something they had heard gypsies did. The Buddicoms' cook discovered the dead hedgehog in her oven and got upset. Another time, the children built a whiskey still that blew up while the cook took her afternoon rest. After this accident, she left her job.

The cook's departure did not change the boys' behavior. Soon they discovered chemical experiments. In one, they made their own gunpowder and sprinkled it in a bonfire, hoping it would explode. When nothing happened, Eric poked it with a stick. The gunpowder exploded, burning their eyebrows and blackening their faces and clothes.

During his last year at St. Cyprian's, Eric had to prepare for entrance examinations for placement in one of the country's prestigious public schools. The first exam he took in February was for Wellington College. He won a scholarship to that school, but he did not want to go there. In the spring an exam for Eton would be given. The exam took two and a half days to complete. He was trying for a King's Scholar placement, one of twelve or thirteen offered each year. Eric placed number fourteen, which meant that he could be accepted to Eton if one of the top thirteen students elected not to attend. Meanwhile, he enrolled at Wellington.

As he finished his five years at St.Cyprian's, he won the Classics Prize and was first runner-up for the Harrow History Prize, which his friend Cyril Connolly won. On the last day at the school, Eric bid farewell to Mrs. Wilkes. She was courteous, but he remembered a look of superiority on her face and a sarcastic tone in her voice. She was convinced her school helped young boys succeed in the academic world. Eric saw St. Cyprian's as a rigid enforcer of class boundaries.

Chapter Two

Sidestepping the University

After nine weeks at Wellington College, fourteen-year-old Eric was granted a scholarship to Eton in March 1917. Here Eric found the same emphasis on class that had plagued him at St. Cyprian's. The school had two categories of students. Oppidans were stereotyped as snobbish sons of the wealthy. They may have been athletic, but they were rarely thought of as highly intelligent or studious. Oppidans were housed off the campus in the town. Eric was a member of the other group, the King's Scholars, also known as Collegers and Tugs, short for togas, which referred to the gowns the boys wore. Collegers were thought of as middle-class boys who had been chosen to attend Eton because they were brainy and studious. They were not as socially polished as the wealthier boys. Their dormitories were on the campus proper. These two groups tended to stay separate.

During his first year, Eric lived in a large room called Chamber with thirteen others in his Election (the other boys who had earned scholarships in the same year). Each boy had a stall containing a desk, chair, bookcase, and folding bed. There were no rugs and only a single fireplace in Chamber. The Sixth Form, boys in their last year, enforced discipline in Chamber by beating rule-breakers with a cane.

If a boy had to be disciplined, a messenger would arrive with the announcement "you're wanted." The victim would put his gown over his school uniform and report. The Sixth Form boys would lecture him and pronounce punishment. The boy would kneel on a chair without his gown to be caned. At the end of the beating, someone in the Sixth Form would say, "Good night," and the victim could go back to Chamber. Eric preferred this ordeal to the one at St. Cyprian's, where the wielders of the cane were adults who operated mainly on whim.

Eric had worked hard at St. Cyprian's, but at Eton he decided to enjoy pleasure reading and not strive so hard to excel. Mr. Gow, Eric's Eton tutor, recalled, "Once he was safely installed at Eton, he had rather given up working: he said he deserved a rest after the intensive effort at St. Cyprian's." Tuesday, Thursday, and Saturday afternoons were times off for the boys. School authorities expected the boys to pursue athletics, but they did not demand it. Eric preferred to read. He devoured works by Jack London, George Bernard Shaw, and H. G. Wells.

The students' attitudes toward World War I were changing as more former Etonians died in action. Initially the boys' image of the soldiers had been of heroes answering the call to patriotic duty. By 1917, with body counts rising, the war carried less appeal. Most students served in the Officer Training Corps, but without dedication. Eric recalled, "To be as slack as you dared on OTC parades, and to take no interest in the war, was considered a mark of enlightenment."

Eric continued to spend holiday times with the Buddicom children. In August 1917 he was a guest at their grandfather's house. Nearly every day the boys went hunting or fishing. Eric was growing taller and losing his childhood chubbiness. During the Christmas recess of 1917, both Eric and his sister Avril stayed at the Buddicom home. Richard Blair, now retired, had been commissioned as a second lieutenant at age sixty and was stationed in France. Mrs. Blair and Marjorie had secured wartime jobs in London. Mrs. Blair paid Mrs. Buddicom to look after her two younger children.

Eric took a romantic interest in Jacintha. In October 1918, the fifteen-year-old boy sent seventeen-year-old Jacintha a love poem. Other poems would follow. When he was away at school, they wrote each other nearly every week, but Jacintha recalled that she "never had a kiss from him, and I didn't try to give him one. It was a kind of mental romantic feeling on his part, and I think I was good-natured about it, but we were not in love."

Classmates from Eton remembered Eric as quiet and not quick to make friends. His manner of speaking made others think that he was emotionally distant. His habits of smoking cigarettes and making fun of boys' parents, his own included, further isolated him.

Some of his friendships began through his involvement in the editing of literary magazines. He worked with Denys King-Farlow on their handwritten *Election Times* and the more polished *College Days*. The two editors actually made some money from the distribution of *College Days*.

Academically, Eric was far from a shining star. In the examinations of the 1920 summer term, he placed 117 out of 140 students. He occupied the lowest spot of all the boys in his Election.

Aldous Huxley, who would write the novel *Brave New World*, substituted as Eric's French teacher when the regular teacher went to fight in the war. Eric and another student enjoyed the class because of Huxley's fascination with unusual words. But Huxley could not maintain order in the classroom, partly because he had poor vision.

Eric continued to grow taller—tall enough in 1918 to be recruited into Eton's informal tradition called the Wall Game. In this adaptation of British football (soccer), teams kicked a ball back and forth against a brick wall 120 yards long in their attempt to score goals. The teams spent most of the time in muddy gridlocks. At first Eric played the position of goalie poorly and indifferently. But by October 1920 he was also playing standard British football, and much more seriously. "The Annals of Foot-Ball" of Eton College recorded on October 6: "The feature of the first half was a superb goal neatly shot by Blair . . . then the keeper scored off a good penalty kick by Blair . . . Blair was confident . . .

Blair kicked very well . . . Blair kicked competently and under considerable pressure."

Eric spent the last week of the 1920 summer term with the Officer Training Corps. Then the seventeen-year-old took a train for the family's vacation at Cornwall. His parents would be there with Avril. By now, Marjorie had married her childhood friend Humphrey Dakin and was living in London. Eric's father had finished his tour of duty with the army, and his mother had left her job in London.

On his way to Cornwall, Eric missed the train and had to spend the night in town. Wearing a military uniform, he was often mistaken for a soldier. He was scared, cold, and hungry. He used the seven pence he had to buy buns and slept in a farmer's field.

This was Eric's first experience with tramping, and it would not be his last. He loved the freedom and anonymity of the adventure. Tramping freed him from middle-class responsibilities. He was no longer E.A. Blair, King's Scholar. Eric always wanted to experiment. As he had made his own gunpowder and rolled his own cigarettes, he was now creating his own adventure.

His last day at Eton was December 20, 1921. He had spent five years at St. Cyprian's and five at Eton. Most Collegers went on to Oxford or Cambridge for university training. Eric's family had no money for this. He had performed poorly and would not receive a scholarship. Furthermore, he was sick of school and wanted new and different experiences. What could the eighteen-year-old do?

Eric and his family decided that he would enter the service of the Indian Imperial Police, following a career similar to that of his father's. In June 1922 he took the Civil Service exam in London. His performance was poor in history and average in English and French. His ranking in Greek and Latin proved superior. A compulsory horseback-riding test brought his score down somewhat, but not far enough to disqualify him. Overall, Eric ranked seventh among twenty-six finalists. In October Eric was given the probationary position of Assistant District Superintendent of Police.

Richard and Ida's reasons for wanting their son to make this career choice were different from Eric's. His parents considered the job realistic: It was a respectable position with adequate income and retirement. "To

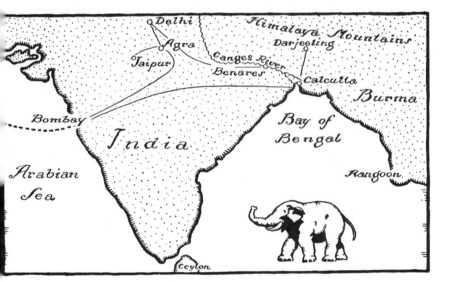

serve King and Country in an Outpost of the Empire carried with it a certain distinction: one was placed, and not discreditably."

Eric, on the other hand, saw the move as an exotic adventure, a return to a unique past, a link with his family history. He had, after all, been born in India. One of his favorite books, Rudyard Kipling's *Kim*, takes place in India. Eric had no way of knowing that by becoming an agent of the British Empire, he was going against his own nature. Yet this step would teach him things about the world that would be essential to his development as a writer.

Burma was his first choice for an assignment. His mother's relatives had a teak business in Burma, and his grandmother still lived there. It was considered an undeveloped section of India with a need for police because of its high crime rate, especially gang murders. At the time, the entire region was unstable because citizens were boycotting British goods and students were conducting strikes. Because of the hardships in Burma, police officers assigned there received a hardship allowance.

Now nineteen, Eric left Liverpool, England, in October, on a five-week boat trip. The ship sailed to Port Said, through the Suez Canal, and into the Red Sea toward Ceylon. Eric witnessed his first sight of imperialism as he watched a white police sergeant kicked an Indian laborer from behind as he struggled to unload a large piece of luggage. No one appeared shocked at the sergeant's treatment of the laborer.

Eric admired the writing of Rudyard Kipling.
(Courtesy of The Library of Congress.)

In November the ship arrived at Rangoon, Burma, on the Irawaddy River. Eric took a train to Mandalay, 100 miles north, where the Provincial Police Training School was located. There he began a two-year training period, involving a year of criminal-law, police-procedure, and language courses in Hindustani and Burmese, followed by a year of field experience.

The Upper Burma Club was a popular gathering place for trainees. Eric stayed away from the club, preferring to read alone in his room. Sometimes he did go on excursions with a fellow trainee named Roger Beadon. They would drive about the countryside on motorcycles. Eric's motorcycle was so low to the ground that his knees reached almost up to his chin. Once, approaching a set of fort gates, Eric realized too late that they were closed. Because he could not stop in time, he stood up, letting the motorcycle barrel ahead and crash into the gates. Eric was not hurt, only embarrassed.

He disliked Mandalay. Eric had heard that it offered five main products: "pagodas, pariahs [the lower castes], pigs, priests, and prostitutes," but he did like some of its less reputable characters. One was a former officer in the British army, Captain H. R. Robinson. He had been forced out of the military, married a Burmese woman, and was now suffering from opium addiction. He claimed to have discovered the secret of the universe in one statement, but after his bouts with opium could never recall it. At last he was able to write the secret down: "The banana is great, but the skin is greater." Robinson

Eric began to hate his job as an Imperial Policeman in Burma.

tried to commit suicide by shooting himself in the head but succeeded only in blinding himself. He later wrote a book about his life. Eric made friends with a former classmate from Eton. He too was an outcast from British society because he had married an Indian woman.

After his training period was over, Eric worked as an assistant police superintendent in five successive districts. In his spare time he did an enormous amount of reading, including Tolstoy's *War and Peace*, D.H. Lawrence's *Women in Love*, and Samuel Butler's *Notebooks*. He also wrote poems and prose sketches about Burmese life. During a British Broadcasting Corporation interview a year later, Roger Beadon commented on Eric's way of living at one post: ". . . he had goats, geese, ducks, and all sorts of things floating about downstairs . . . it didn't worry him what the house looked like."

Eric's first posting was at Myaungmya in the Irawaddy Delta. He ran the office at the district headquarters, supervised storage areas and records, organized the training school, oversaw the headquarters staff, arranged escorts for court sessions, oversaw night patrols, and took over when his supervisor had to travel out of the area. These were considerable responsibilities for a young man in his early twenties. His next posting was farther east in the same delta. His third put him in charge of security at a large oil refinery. This work was less demanding, and he was located only ten miles from the city of Rangoon.

On a visit to Rangoon one day, Eric was wearing

civilian clothes. He was walking toward a train station, when a schoolboy bumped against him, pushing him off balance. Angrily, Eric hit the boy's back with his walking stick. Some university students came to the boy's defense and argued with Eric about his conduct. When Eric's train arrived, the group continued their argument inside the car. Eventually, everyone settled the dispute and parted. Eric never informed the protestors that he was a policeman. The boys learned that later. Perhaps he knew that he could settle the dispute more easily if he were not identified as part of the controlling elite in the country. Already, he felt some shame about his function in Burma.

Eric tried hard to be the model policeman. But many things worked against him—"loneliness, boredom, and physical discomfort." He began attending services in Burmese temples and conversing with priests in their own language. A fellow policeman remembered that Eric "did not seem happy but [I] did not know what the trouble was." Eric felt pulled between his responsibility toward the British Empire and his empathy with the Burmese.

By the time Eric left his post at Insein in 1926, he realized he could not continue as an Imperial policeman. It was obvious to him that imperialism caused the mistreatment of the Burmese. Less obvious but becoming clearer was the damage done to the British as well. Years later, in his essay "Shooting an Elephant," Eric wrote, "In Moulmein, in Lower Burma, I was hated by large numbers of people—the only time in my life that I have been important enough for this to happen to me." Eric later realized that imperialism left no room for compassion on either side. He was "haunted by all the misery he had seen—the frightened looks in the eyes of men who had been condemned to suffer execution, the ugly scars on the backs of men who had been flogged in prison, the pathetic cries of women whose husbands had been taken away . . . in handcuffs."

Eric was struck with a dilemma. "Give an inch to the Burmese, and you betray your white brothers; turn your back on the just claims of the Burmese, and you lose your sense of moral integrity." From Insein, he went on to serve at Moulmein and then Katha before returning to England on sick leave in the summer of 1927. In Katha he had contracted a tropical disease called dengue fever. Slated for a leave soon anyway, he left early because of his illness.

During the boat trip home, Eric had time to reflect on whether he should resign from the Imperial police. He later wrote, "Unfortunately, I had not trained myself to be indifferent to the expression of the human face."

Chapter Three

Struggling Writer

Arriving home in August 1927 after a brief stay in France, Eric felt relieved to be able to say what he was thinking without fearing the reactions of his superiors. His relatives were struck by the change in his appearance. He had grown a small moustache, and he was noticeably thinner. At his request the entire family took a vacation in Cornwall until September. During this vacation, Eric told his mother that he had resigned from the Imperial police. He also told his parents that he intended to become a writer. A friend of the family, Mabel Fierz, observed that "his father was very disappointed and looked upon him as some sort of failure . . . His mother . . . said to me, 'You know, Eric loves his father more than he loves me.' And I said, 'No, I don't think he does—he wants his father to acknowledge him as a successful son.' The son who couldn't make money in old Mr. Blair's concept was not the right sort of son."

Eric used up his sick leave, making his resignation effective on January 1, 1928. His new life gave him little or no income, but he felt that this was a fair trade-off. Brenda Salkeld, a close friend later in Blair's life, observed: "In the Indian Police he'd made two thousand pounds, but he hated it, and he thought perhaps if he could find something he loathed still more, he might become quite rich."

The aspiring writer wrote Ruth Pitter, a London poet and family friend, asking her to help him get lodging in London. She found him a room next to her employer's workshop. Once he had moved to London, Ruth remembered getting angry with him because he would go out into the cold wearing no coat, gloves, or hat. When she admonished him to take care of his health, he ignored her. Eric shared some of his poems and short stories with Ruth. She showed him his faults with rhythm in his poetry, but she also encouraged him to write more prose. She found his short stories "awkward and contrived."

Eric's landlady had once worked for a nobleman, so she thought herself too refined to associate with the neighbors. On one occasion she was locked out of the house, but she refused to go next door for a ladder. Eric and her husband had to walk nearly a mile to a relative to fetch a ladder.

Eric hardly considered himself too refined. He began disguising himself as a tramp and visiting London's East End so he could know firsthand how the poor lived. His first trip lasted two or three days. The practice would continue intermittently during the next two or three years. He was searching for writing ideas, much as Jack London had done for his *People of the Abyss*, with which Eric was quite familiar. Because Eric had rejected any form of hierarchy within society, he now wanted to experience the downtrodden life that inspired such sympathy in him. Later, his editor and friend Sir Richard Rees said of him, ". . . whether he wrote of poverty or of political persecution, [Eric] was always talking of what he knew about from personal experience."

In the spring of 1928, Eric decided to make a bold move and go to Paris. He found a room with thin walls, plenty of dirt, and numerous insects in a dilapidated hotel. His aunt, Nellie Limouzin, lived in Paris. Somewhat of an eccentric herself, she gave Eric small amounts of money when she could. Eric pursued writing in earnest in Paris and, for a time, was able to publish some of his essays.

In March Eric coughed up blood and developed a temperature of 103 degrees Fahrenheit. He was forced to spend three weeks in a hospital, where doctors discovered pneumonia but, luckily, no sign of tuberculosis, a deadly lung disease. Conditions at the hospital were very harsh. Although he was quite sick upon arrival, he had to answer questions for twenty minutes before he could be admitted. He was put in a ward with sixty other men. At that time, it was believed that sickness could be removed through the blood. Doctors used a cupping glass to raise and break blisters on Eric's skin, drawing out what was considered poisoned blood. Then a mustard poultice was applied to these wounds, which was extremely painful. As this was a teaching hospital, he sometimes had as many as twelve students standing in line to hear his chest rattle. Later he captured his hospital experiences in the essay "How the Poor Die."

In the future, when he became ill, Eric tried to avoid doctors and hospitals. He disliked their cold, impersonal nature. "I had never been in the public ward of a hospital before, and it was my first experience of doctors who handle you without speaking to you, or, in a human sense, taking any notice of you," he wrote.

The day the hospital released Eric, an editor of a French publication relayed to him the news that one of his articles about Burma and the perils of British imperialism would be published. The Burma piece was the most important article Eric published while in Paris.

As money problems increased, Eric and a friend went hungry for three days and were forced to pawn their overcoats. He found a position as a dishwasher and porter in one of the better Parisian hotels. Once, a rich hotel patron requested a single peach. As there were no peaches in the hotel, Eric was told to go find a peach and not to return without one or he would be fired. All the stores were closed. Finally he saw a small shop with a basket of peaches sitting on display in the window. He tried gaining entry to the shop, but it was closed and its proprietor was away. Desperate to keep his job, Eric tossed a rock through the window, then ran off with a single peach.

Later, Eric and his friend quit their jobs at the hotel and found work at a restaurant that primarily employed

Russians. Conditions there were no better. Desperate, Eric wrote another friend in London about the possibility of finding work there. The friend secured a job for Eric, watching over a mentally handicapped person. He even sent Eric money so he could retrieve his clothes from the pawnshop and get a train ticket. He returned to England just before Christmas 1929.

Once back in London, Eric began publishing articles in a magazine called *Adelphi*. Its editors, Sir Richard Rees and Max Plowman, also sent him books to review. He began developing his own voice, with a straightforward, clear language. He continued to work in the journalistic-fiction mode, in essays that emphasized dramatic dialogues, settings, and character development. He was trying to combine factual observation with commentary. He also experimented with conveying two points of view in one piece—one as observer and the other as the person being observed.

To save expense, he stayed with his parents back at Southwold. During school holidays, when Eric finished tutoring the mentally handicapped boy, he worked with the three sons of one of his mother's friends. The boys liked Eric because he behaved like one of them rather than as a teacher.

In the early 1930s Eric became friends with Brenda Salkeld. They walked in the countryside, went horseback riding, and discussed books. He loved to see the shocked look on her face when he related some strange fact or observation. After one of his tramping expeditions, he appeared at her door so disheveled that she made him go right in and take a bath. Sometimes he showed her his writings and asked for her comments. He once wrote a letter to her in which he said that a song becomes something different once it has been created. It continues to live through the years, but in different ways with different meanings and for different purposes. He compared a song to an idea, which also changes as it goes through time. At some point he declared his love for her and proposed marriage, but she rejected his offer. There is some question whether Eric was sincere in his proposal or was just teasing Brenda. They remained friends the rest of his life.

Eric enjoyed painting. He rendered landscapes in and around Southwold. One day, while engaged in this pastime, he met Mabel Fierz and her husband, Francis, who were vacationing in Southwold. Having an interest in writing and writers, Mabel took up Eric's cause, introducing him to her writer friends and urging him to live in London, the hub of the writing community.

Eric borrowed a pair of Francis Fierz's old pants and rubbed them in garden dirt to make them part of his tramp's uniform. He planned to work on a hop farm in Kent for eighteen days with an average workday of ten hours. His hands were stained dark and became cracked and cut by the vines.

About this time he also submitted his first book-length manuscript, *A Scullion's Diary*, to the publisher Jonathan Cape. The book was based on his tramping and transient experiences in London and Paris. Cape rejected it. The editors told him that it was "too short and fragmentary." Even after making revisions and re-submitting the manuscript, he received a second rejection. Eric became concerned and went to his friend, Richard Rees. Rees promised to recommend it to the poet and editor T. S. Eliot of Faber & Faber. Based on Rees's promise, Eric submitted the manuscript to Faber & Faber in December 1930. Eric was worried that his manuscript would be rejected, and that if it were, he would be a failure. His fears led to an eight-month period of severe negativity about his writing, making him believe that everything he did would fail.

Eric submitted *A Scullion's Diary* to T. S. Eliot at Faber & Faber. Eliot was the author of the celebrated poem *The Waste Land.*

The Blair family had never been in the habit of celebrating Christmas together, and the Christmas of 1930 was no exception. Continuing to pursue his interest in writing about the poor, Eric planned to spend Christmas in prison by getting arrested for public drunkenness. He began one night about a week before the holiday by drinking four or five pints of beer and a quarter bottle of whiskey. He did succeed in getting arrested, but only for two days. When he tried a second time, he was not even arrested. Then he begged on the streets, which was also against the law, but the police again ignored him.

About this time, T. S. Eliot rejected *A Scullion's Diary*. This news so discouraged Eric that he gave the manuscript to Mabel Fierz with instructions to dispose of it and keep the paper clips. Mabel liked what she read. In April 1932 she tried to get it published for Eric by approaching the literary agent Leonard Moore and pressuring him to read it. In turn, Moore contacted Eric with the news that he might find him a publisher.

Chapter Four

Reluctant Teacher

Soon money became tight, and Eric was forced to seek employment. He obtained a teaching position at a small school in Hayes, outside London, called the Hawthorns High School for Boys. After spending a couple of months settling in, Eric complained to friends about the school's lock step methods and the provincialism of the community. In his spare time he enjoyed visiting an old church and its adjoining churchyard. He became friends with the minister and even attended some services, although he worried that his minister friend would want him to take communion. How could Eric, a nonbeliever, go through that ritual? Fortunately, Eric never had to face the problem.

One student remembered Eric as strict inside the classroom but approachable outside. He enjoyed sharing his knowledge of art and natural history with his pupils. He directed, wrote, and produced a school play and even made the costumes. He fashioned suits of armor from brown wrapping paper. Another student recalled that putting on the play was great fun, but Eric told his new agent, Leonard Moore, "The miserable school play over which I had wasted so much time went off not badly."

At the end of Eric's first teaching year, the publisher Victor Gollancz informed him that he would accept *A Scullion's Diary* if some changes were made to avoid legal problems of obscenity and libel against businesses and people described in the book. Victor Gollancz, a Socialist, was attracted to the way Eric's book dealt with social inequities.

During the summer months Eric and his sister Avril stayed at the family home in Southwold while their parents visited Marjorie, who now lived in northern England. One day Avril came home from work and saw that Eric had tried to make a distillery using rubber tubing. The liquor he distilled retained the offensive taste of the rubber.

That summer Eric dated Eleanor Jaques, whom he had known in Southwold. They spent days in the country, sometimes picnicking on a beach in the afternoon. Gradually they became very close. Their romance was complicated by Dennis Collings, a good friend of Eric's, who also admired Eleanor. Unfortunately for Dennis, he was away working for the summer while Eleanor and Eric enjoyed one another's company.

As Eric's first book neared publication, now retitled *Down and Out in Paris and London*, he became convinced to use a pen name, or pseudonym, because of potential problems with libel. He also was not proud of the writing. His publisher, Victor Gollancz, suggested the name X, but Eric sent him four other possibilities— P.S. Burton, Kenneth Miles, George Orwell, and H. Lewis Allways, claiming Orwell as his preference. George was a very strong English name, and Orwell was simply the name of a nearby river. He would continue to use the pen name George Orwell except for magazine articles, which he wrote as Eric Blair until 1934.

Down and Out in Paris and London was a long auto-biographical essay. The first part described the ten weeks he had stayed in Paris in 1929, where he was employed some of the time as a dishwasher in a hotel. The second part dealt with his move to London, where he spent time living with the transient poor. It is likely that in some way, Eric was working to purge himself of guilt associated with his brief career as an Imperial policeman. In Burma he had viewed poverty from the distance of his class, but in Paris he lived among the poor, as the poor lived. He described the experience of hunger and showed how far one will go to hide one's poverty. He also detailed the dirty kitchens of the finest Parisian hotels.

When *Down and Out in Paris and London* was published in January 1933, it received favorable reviews. However, it was more a series of sketches rather than a single narrative. The two sections, Paris and London, were not closely related, either. Nevertheless, some of the descriptive passages made up for this disunity. One such passage described the crippled pavement artist, Bozo, who struggled to remain free of others' pity and domination.

When they read the book, Orwell's parents were surprised that their rather distant son showed himself to be quite open concerning some matters—sex, for example. Orwell never felt comfortable discussing his family or childhood, but he seemed willing to make other experiences available to the public. As flattering as the reviews were, Orwell still had trouble getting his parents' approval. He also found it necessary to continue teaching in Hayes for added income.

A Paris hotelier wrote a letter to the editor of the *Times Literary Supplement*. He claimed that kitchens in better hotels were quite clean, unlike the kitchens portrayed in the book. Orwell replied with a letter of his own, stating, "I do know that in our hotel there were places which no customer could possibly have been allowed to see with any hope of retaining his custom."

Orwell's agent, Leonard Moore, continued his efforts to find an American publisher for *Down and Out*. Finally he landed an acceptance with Harper & Brothers. When the book was published, American reviews were complimentary. Meanwhile, Orwell worked on a novel about his experiences in Burma. Moore encouraged him to continue once he saw the opening chapters.

Despite a busy teaching and writing schedule, Orwell managed to plant a small vegetable garden behind his school, where he grew broad beans, shallots, peas, potatoes, and a pumpkin. He also continued meeting with Eleanor. But at the end of July 1932, when she had not responded to a letter of his, he discovered that Eleanor wanted more than a casual relationship—she wanted marriage. Orwell's busy life made this impossible. Her other admirer, Dennis Collings, was beginning a career with the Colonial Service. She and Dennis married in September, and towards the end of 1934 they left for his first duty post in Singapore.

Orwell found it difficult to juggle the demands of writing and teaching. He secured a new position teaching French at Frays College, a few miles north of Hawthorns. It was a larger school, with 200 pupils and a staff of sixteen. Orwell kept to himself, taking long motorcycle rides in the country with only a sport coat for warmth.

By December 1934, he had completed his 400-page manuscript of *Burmese Days*, which he delivered to Moore. Orwell was not satisfied with the work, but he was frustrated with trying to fix it and wanted to be relieved of the burden. He later recalled: "I wanted to write enormous naturalistic novels with unhappy endings, full of detailed descriptions and arresting similes, and also full of purple passages in which words were used partly for the sake of their sound. And in fact my first complete novel, *Burmese Days* . . . is rather that kind of book."

The book dealt with a man's self-hatred as he lives the false and risky life of an imperialist. Orwell's book identified with the peasants at the mercy of the powerful. The ideas had been taking shape in his mind since his return from Burma. Writing about the experience allowed him to fictionally retrace those painful steps in his first career.

In the middle of December Orwell caught a chill after riding his motorcycle in an ice storm. The chill led to pneumonia, and Orwell had to enter the nearest hospital. The first few days were serious. His mother and Avril hurried to visit, but by the time they arrived, he was getting better. During his delirium, he spoke constantly of money, saying he wished he had some under his pillow. Orwell may have been thinking of his tramping days, when safe money was very important and travelers often slept with it under their heads. This was Orwell's fourth bout with pneumonia.

Orwell returned to his family's home after release from the hospital in January 1934. His family advised that he end his teaching career and undergo a period of rest. This idea appealed to him because it would give him more time for his writing.

Gollancz decided not to publish *Burmese Days* because he feared lawsuits for libel. However, the American publisher Harper Brothers would take a chance on the book, providing certain changes were made. Orwell signed the contract in March.

By spring he was working on another novel, *A Clergyman's Daughter*. He also enjoyed walks along the beach or by a river. One day he impulsively took off his clothes and went swimming in what he thought was a deserted area. While he was swimming, several people came by, including a member of the Coast Guard. To avoid being arrested for public nudity, Orwell had to swim for another half hour until the people finally went away.

All along, Orwell had been feeling that his writing was no good, and *A Clergyman's Daughter* was coming along no differently. He was reading James Joyce's *Ulysses* at the time. Joyce was a poet and novelist from Dublin, Ireland, who moved to Italy and broke from Irish literary tradition. He experimented with both language and style, including *stream of consciousness* writing. This style foregoes conventional sentence structure and concentrates instead on the way the human mind wanders. Joyce's long autobiographical novel

Orwell experimented with writing techniques that he learned from reading the works of James Joyce. *(Courtesy of The Library of Congress.)*

Ulysses, published in Paris in 1922, is filled with this kind of language experimentation. Orwell admired the book's dual perspective, which allowed readers to experience events from both inside and outside a character. He attempted some of Joyce's techniques in *A Clergyman's Daughter*.

Orwell was working toward being more imaginative in his writing style, but he felt most comfortable depending on his own life experiences to form the plot in his novels. In *A Clergyman's Daughter*, for example, he included a detailed account of directing and producing a school play. This reluctance to leave the real world behind may have been partly due to lack of confidence, but he wanted to share his real-life experiences with others. "I am not a real novelist," he confided to a friend. "One difficulty I have never solved is that one has masses of experience which one passionately wants to write about . . . and no way of using them up except by disguising them in a novel." This dilemma would persist through all of his books except *Animal Farm*.

Chapter Five

The Making of a Socialist

Orwell finished *A Clergyman's Daughter* in October 1934 and sent it to Moore, although he was doubtful about its success. Now that he was unemployed, his aunt Nellie Limouzin came to Orwell's rescue once again. She contacted some friends in London who owned a second-hand bookshop, Booklovers' Corner. They agreed to give Orwell a part-time job and to let him live in the room above the shop.

Booklovers' Corner had two rooms—one with second-hand books for sale and another with a lending library. Orwell enjoyed reading the strange books and observing the people who searched through them. The shop's customers included people who just chanced to wander in to pass some time, those who got into the way of others, browsers intent on finding good books, thieves, and the mentally ill.

While Orwell was setting himself up in London, *Burmese Days* was published. During the following one and a half months, the book received only one review, which was negative. Some favorable reviews were eventually published, including one in the *New York Times*. A review in the *Boston Evening Transcript* claimed that the main character was masterfully developed. But reviews were not enough to save *Burmese Days*. Four months after publication in America, the publisher took it out of print.

Gollancz looked at the manuscript for *A Clergyman's Daughter,* nervously worried again about libel problems. When he finally requested changes, it took Orwell nearly a month to make them. He also asked Gollancz to include *Burmese Days* on the list of "Books by the Same Author" on the book's jacket. Shortly afterwards, Gollancz asked to see the manuscript for *Burmese Days* again, even though he had already rejected it once. This time, after some libel problems had been cleared up, Gollancz decided to publish it.

Orwell continued working at Booklovers' Corner, but he moved his lodgings to Parliament Hill, a place Mabel Fierz had recommended, where he shared the apartment with two women, Rosalind Obermeyer and Janet Gimson. Orwell's room was filthy. Food rotted in the back of his cupboard, and then mice took over. At night the housemates could hear them rummaging around for scraps.

Orwell wrote for three hours each morning before going to work at Booklovers' Corner, then again in the evening unless he had other plans. Often in the evening he would entertain friends by cooking for them. At this time he was making more friends in the literary world.

One was the poet Dylan Thomas, and another was a writer named Rayner Heppenstall. Heppenstall remembered that Orwell was "a tall, big-headed man, with pale-blue, defensively humorous eyes, a little moustache and a painfully snickering laugh." He thought Orwell an odd individual with several prejudices, particularly against Scots and Catholics. While Orwell was often quiet, when he talked about a topic that interested him, getting a word into his monologues was difficult.

A Clergyman's Daughter hit the bookstores in March 1935. The novel follows a daughter, suffering from amnesia, who travels to London, the hopfields of Kent, and back to London. From there she returns to her father's rectory a changed woman because of her experiences. The adventure has helped her to know herself better. The book also examines faith and hypocrisy.

By now Orwell was at work on *Keep the Aspidistra Flying,* based in part on his experiences in the bookstore. The book would explore the corrupting influence that money had on people's lives. The main character, Gordon Comstock, tries to remain true to his convictions and claim voluntary poverty after examining and denouncing a society based on money. But events have a way of pulling him back into the money game. Complain as he might, he becomes like everyone else.

Once good reviews of *A Clergyman's Daughter* were received, Orwell felt confident—so much so, in fact, that he and his housemates held a party for about a dozen people. He invited Richard Rees and Heppenstall, and his roommate, Rosalind, invited some of her friends.

Rosalind's guest Eileen Maud O'Shaughnessy was of interest to Orwell. He spent most of the evening talking with her. Eileen had large shoulders and brown hair. She had taught in a private boarding school for girls but left after one term to go into social work, and then gave that up to buy and run a London secretarial agency. She later decided to sell the agency and return to college for a graduate degree in educational psychology. After the party, Orwell told Rosalind that he had found the type of girl he could marry.

A few days later he took Eileen horseback riding. A few weeks later, she told a friend that he had asked her to marry him. The friend asked what she intended to do about the proposal, and she responded: "I don't know . . . You see, I told myself that when I was 30 I would accept the first man who asked me to marry him." She would soon be turning thirty.

In many ways Eileen was a good match for Orwell. She was a perceptive reader and critic. She also could tactfully tone down or even contradict his more outrageous statements. Orwell repeated his proposal of marriage on several other occasions.

When *Burmese Days* came out in England in June 1935, his old friend from St. Cyprian's, Cyril Connolly, gave it a positive review, and the two renewed their friendship shortly afterwards. Connolly was shocked to see that the thirty-two-year-old looked ravaged and sick. Orwell's careless handling of his health and his repeated bouts with pneumonia were taking their toll.

In October 1935 Orwell gave a lecture called "Confessions of a Down and Out" to the South Woodford Literary Society. The large audience of between 400 and 500 people received his talk well. He spoke for over an hour. A reporter from the *Woodford Times* wrote of the event:

> Mr. Orwell . . . said that many people were apt to regard a destitute man as a rogue who needed discouraging as much as possible, and he did not think much could be done in the way of improvement until people realised that they were human beings like the rest of the community, driven by the force of circumstances to lead this wretched life.

Orwell hoped that the success of this event would lead to more lecture engagements.

The upcoming author moved again—this time from his lodgings with the two women at Parliament Hill to Lawford Road, where he kept bachelor quarters with his friend Heppenstall and another struggling writer, Michael Sayers. This move was not without its problems. For one thing, Heppenstall fell behind in his rent payments, and Orwell was forced to pay for him so that they would not lose their lease.

A particular incident forced Heppenstall abruptly out of the apartment. One night he came home drunk and woke Orwell, who lectured him about his crude behavior. The two exchanged verbal, then physical blows. When he finally got into his bedroom, Heppenstall heard a key turn, locking him in. He became so furious that he started kicking out the door panels. Orwell unlocked the door, opened it, and stood there with a shooting stick, a cane with a flat handle. He pushed Heppenstall back into the room with it, hit the man's legs, then left. Before the blow with the stick, Heppenstall recalled, "Through my private mists I saw in [Orwell's face] a curious blend of fear and sadistic exaltation." The next day Orwell ordered Heppenstall out of the house.

Some critics have pointed to this incident and the time Orwell beat the Burmese student as evidence of Orwell's cruel streak, in order to explain some aspects of his writing. But Mabel Fierz, who knew both men well, later remembered that Heppenstall could be extremely difficult at times and was especially so that night. A year after the incident, the two men resolved their differences and became friends once more. While Orwell did often employ a sardonic sense of humor both among his friends and in his writing, he successfully resolved matters and established peace. Most relationships with his other acquaintances remained friendly, as well.

Europe was undergoing upheaval in the mid-1930s. After World War I, Socialism had become increasingly popular, threatening the stability of the middle and upper classes. In Italy, panic-stricken businessmen retaliated by embracing Fascism to stop government take-over of their properties. By 1922, Benito Mussolini and his Fascist followers were in control of the Italian government. The Fascists believed in three measures: totalitarianism, meaning the state demands full allegiance of its citizens; nationalism, meaning the nation is the supreme form of human society; and militarism, meaning nations must expand their boundaries to remain healthy. In 1936 Mussolini tried to focus Italian citizens' attention away from their poor economic conditions by conquering the North African country of Ethiopia. As Fascism captured the attention of Europe, Orwell became more focused on politics. He decided Socialism was Fascism's most viable enemy.

Change in world events was prompting a change in George Orwell's writing. *Keep the Aspidistra Flying* had focused on an individual's attempt to act out his own social philosophy. Now he was interested in how groups of people interact. In an essay titled "Why I Write," he looked back on that transition:

> What I have most wanted to do throughout the past ten years is to make political writing into an art. My starting point is always a feeling of partisanship, a sense of injustice. When I sit down to write a book, I do not say to myself, 'I am going to produce a work of art.' I write it because there is some lie that I want to expose, some fact to which I want to draw attention, and my initial concern is to get a hearing.

It became increasingly true that when George Orwell had a political purpose, his writing took on life.

When Orwell hand-delivered the manuscript of *Keep the Aspidistra Flying* in January 1936, Gollancz suggested a new book which appealed to Orwell's new political sensibilities—writing about unemployment and living conditions in northern England. Although Orwell knew he would miss Eileen, he felt comfortable leaving for a short period. He left his apartment and bookstore job, said good-bye to Eileen, and headed north.

His first contact was Frank Meade, a trade-union official in Manchester. He suggested that Orwell visit the town of Wigan and Joe "Jerry" Kennan, a mine electrician there. Orwell's first lodgings were above a tripe shop (a store that sold food made from cow's stomach). Conditions were so slovenly that he got another living arrangement after only two weeks.

The trips down into the mines proved hard on Orwell physically. Because of his height, he had to bend at the waist and knees for miles on end. In addition, the coal dust was bad for his already sensitive lungs. Nevertheless, he endured the hardships so he could see the difficulties and dangers miners faced daily. Sometimes explosions injured or killed workers. At other times, loose debris fell on them. There were also cage malfunctions, where the cars in which men traveled to or from the surface plunged downward, killing the workers inside.

Orwell talked with miners and their families and visited their workplaces. He also spent time collecting statistics in the public library. For example, he discovered that between 1927 and 1934, 8000 men had died in the mines. Every year one in each group of 900 was killed, one in six injured. These figures did not even take into account the detrimental effect of coal dust on the lungs and eyes. And, because of a housing shortage, workers were forced to live in slums, similar to those in a refugee camp.

Orwell also briefly visited the Liverpool docks and South Yorkshire, where he went to Communist and Fascist public meetings. He began to realize that political problems lay behind poverty, and these needed to be addressed to correct the situation in northern England.

He finished his visit to the North on March 30 and returned to London. As soon as he had met with his publisher and visited Eileen, he went back thirty-five miles north to investigate a small cottage for rent in Wallington. He rented the house and moved in on the first of April. Wallington was a small community. It contained thirty-four houses, two bars, and a single church. As he was writing his manuscript for his book on the North, *The Road to Wigan Pier*, he re-opened and ran the small grocery store that had occupied the front of the cottage years earlier. Much of his business came from children in search of penny candy. Orwell hoped the country cottage would entice Eileen to marry him.

Beyond the front room on the first floor, which served as the store, was a sitting room. Orwell used this as his study. There was also a small kitchen. Upstairs were two bedrooms. The front door stood only four feet high, which was a real nuisance for tall George.

Outside were gently rolling hills, and a small pond sat about 100 yards from the front door. The next town was three miles distant. Orwell's only transportation was a bicycle. He had no electricity, no tap water, and only an outdoor lavatory.

In April Gollancz brought out *Keep the Aspidistra Flying*. Reviews were far from glowing, and sales were limited. Orwell's friend Cyril Connolly wrote a review in which he said, "The writer of *Burmese Days* was . . . fond of Burma and included many beautiful descriptions of it, while the writer of *Keep the Aspidistra Flying* hates London and everything there." Orwell was apparently undisturbed at public response to the novel. He himself called it "a silly potboiler."

Chapter Six

Marriage and War

In June 1936, Orwell's numerous proposals paid off. At the age of thirty-three, he married Eileen, age thirty, in a church not far from Wallington. The two were not churchgoers, but he wanted a conventional ceremony. The day of his wedding, Orwell wrote to a former schoolmate, Denys King-Farlow:

> I'm afraid I can't possibly come along on the 11th, much as I would like to, first of all because it's always difficult for me to get away from here, secondly because . . . I have married a wife and therefore I cannot come. Curiously enough I am getting married this very morning—in fact I am writing this with one eye on the clock and the other on the Prayer Book, which I have been studying for some days past in hopes of steeling myself against the obscenities of the wedding service.

Eileen and George walked to the church from the cottage. Orwell jumped over the church wall so that he could carry Eileen from the gate to the church door, a unique version of carrying a bride across the threshold of her new home. Mr. and Mrs. Blair and Avril were in attendance, as were Eileen's brother, Laurence, and his wife, Gwen O'Shaughnessy. Eileen's mother was also in attendance. Eric's father and Eileen's mother served as witnesses during the ceremony.

After the ceremony, a reception was held at the cottage. Orwell's mother and sister told Eileen that they were sorry for her, as she had taken on a considerable challenge in George Orwell. Someone had given a pot of marmalade as a gift, which Eileen placed on the table. Orwell put up a fuss, claiming that the marmalade should be put into a jam dish. When Eileen explained that they did not own one, he claimed that they would soon get one. This concern for middle-class propriety amused Eileen, who had been told often by Orwell that they would be living the working-class life.

The cottage was sparsely furnished, and the chimney was forever giving out smoke. Lopsided door and window frames made for a drafty dwelling, even in warmer weather. Friends who stayed on the second floor were bothered by birds nesting between the ceiling and the roof. At night the birds made considerable noise.

Two days after the wedding, Orwell sent his essay "Shooting an Elephant," a critique of imperialism based on his days in Burma, to the editor of *New Writing*. Eileen seemed to have a mellowing effect on his writing. Compared to his earlier work, this essay was more humane and complex.

Orwell married Eileen Maud O'Shaughnessy in June 1936.
(Courtesy of University College London.,

The couple wasted no time tackling a garden. They planted apple and plum trees, gooseberry bushes, and roses. They kept goats and chickens and started a vegetable garden. Afternoons were very quiet. This country life was peaceful, but world events would soon intrude.

Orwell continued to work away at *The Road to Wigan Pier*, finishing a draft in October. In early summer, Spanish workers rebelled against General Franco and his troops, who had overthrown the elected government. This event came in the wake of a recent Fascist takeover in Abyssinia and the steady advance of Germany's Nazism.

A now politically alert Orwell wanted to view the Spanish rebellion and perhaps even participate in it. Meanwhile, he completed and submitted the manuscript of *The Road to Wigan Pier* in mid-December. This freed him up to become more serious about a trip to Spain.

When *The Road to Wigan Pier* was published, leftist writers criticized it because they felt Orwell had not let the facts speak but instead had inserted himself into the narrative. Later critics rejoiced in the personal commentary because they could learn more about the man, including his nostalgia for childhood days and his fascination with Britain's greatness as an imperial power. These personal touches helped draw readers to his ideas. *The Road to Wigan Pier* was Orwell's first conscious attempt to "make political writing into an art."

Gollancz chose *The Road to Wigan Pier* as a Left Book Club publication, which increased circulation and sales. In fact, this book sold better than all Orwell's previous books combined.

As he prepared for his trip to Spain, Orwell doubted that he could qualify to fight because of his weak lungs. While he waited for clearance, he knew he could do correspondence work for a magazine. Before leaving, he secured a letter of introduction from the International Labor Party (ILP) to its Barcelona branch in Spain. He went first to Paris, then to the Spanish border.

In Barcelona, Orwell found John McNair of the ILP. He joined its military branch, the POUM, or the Workers' Party of Marxist Unification, then spent a week at the barracks practicing parade-ground drills. Because of Orwell's large feet, McNair had to order two pairs of size twelve boots from England. At the beginning of January, Orwell received permission to fight on the front lines, and he stayed with the fighting unit almost four months.

Orwell's captain promoted him to corporal because of his facility with languages. The rifle he finally received came from the 1890s. At that time the weather was very cold with a lot of ice and wind. A firewood shortage made living conditions even worse. In eighty days, he could take his clothes off only three times. Orwell tried to keep his mind off the cold by reciting favorite poems he knew, such as Gerard Manley Hopkins's "Felix Randal."

Despite hardships, Orwell was impressed with the democratic spirit in the troops. Class ranks seemed to have disappeared, and the troops addressed one another as "comrade." There were officers, but no strict military rank as is usually found in armies. All the members of Orwell's unit earned the same pay and shared in the same amenities. All men were equal.

Even though they were at the front lines, Orwell and his comrades found daily life boring. For relief, they sometimes undertook grave risks. One of Orwell's fellow soldiers, Bob Edwards, reflected: "Blair is a fine type of Englishman, 6 feet 3 inches in height, a good shot, a cool customer, completely without fear. I know this because we have on numerous occasions crept over the parapet and have managed to get very close to the Fascist lines." Some felt Orwell took too many risks. An Irishman who fought with him had that opinion. He also remembered Orwell writing all the time and smoking strong, black tobacco.

To be closer to her husband, Eileen began working at the ILP headquarters in Barcelona. Orwell's Aunt Nellie from France agreed to look after their cottage and grocery shop in Wallington while they were away. When Eileen could arrange it, she visited Orwell at the front.

During one night raid, a fellow soldier recalled that although Orwell proved to be bright, rational, and brave, his comrade "was afraid for him. He was so tall and always standing up. I tell him, 'Keep your head down,' but he is always standing up." Another comrade remembered that Orwell led the attack that night, with grenades going off all around. "Orwell stood up, very tall, and shouted, 'Come on, move up here . . . ' "

Orwell served on the Aragon front for 115 days. He

Orwell traveled to Spain to participate in that country's civil war.
(Courtesy of The Library of Congress.)

obtained leave toward the end of April 1937. When he arrived in Barcelona, Eileen noticed the change: "He arrived completely ragged, almost barefoot, a little lousy [having lice], dark brown, and looking really very well."

Unhappy that his unit had not seen more fighting action, Orwell applied to serve with the International Brigade, a Communist unit. The group granted him permission, but something happened to change Orwell's mind about the Brigade.

In early May, aided by the Communists, government troops resisting Franco's overthrow tried to get control of the telephone system, which was being run by a group called the Anarchists, who were closely allied to the POUM. After three days of shooting in Barcelona, the struggle ended, and the telephone system stayed in Anarchist hands. But Orwell "could not join any Communist-controlled unit," since the Communists had gone against his outfit, the POUM.

Back at the front in mid-May, Orwell stood on a sandbag to look over a wall. Suddenly a shot hit him. The bullet had gone into his throat. Medics immediately carried him on a stretcher to a small hospital, then to a larger one, giving him morphine to ease the pain. At the second hospital, he improved quickly, although his voice remained whispery for many weeks. At a third hospital, he was allowed daily walks in the garden. When Eileen visited him, she arranged for him to move to Barcelona once he was strong enough. She also contacted her brother, Laurence, who was a doctor, to see if he could help by reviewing Orwell's prognosis.

By June he was much better, although he felt depressed because for him the war seemed over. Soviet officials declared the POUM an enemy, and thus the Madrid government declared its members illegal Fascists. Many members were harassed and jailed, and some were even executed. The Orwells lived every day at risk. Eileen returned to her apartment and kept a low profile, while George returned to a tramping life to avoid officials. Although away from the front lines, Orwell took what might be considered foolish chances. Hearing a friend and fellow soldier, Georges Kopp, had been arrested, George and Eileen bravely visited the jail in an attempt to free him. The police had seized an official letter stating that Kopp, a Belgian, was free to fight in Spain. Orwell left Eileen at the jail and went to police headquarters, where he managed to obtain the letter. Although the police still refused to free Georges Kopp, Orwell had been willing to sacrifice his own freedom to free his friend. The authorities kept Kopp jailed another eighteen months.

Chapter Seven

Illness Haunts

Orwell and Eileen escaped from Barcelona on June 23. They went by train directly to France. Eileen wanted to go home to England, but Orwell felt that first they needed a vacation along the French coast. The weather was unpleasant. Also, they found it difficult separating themselves from the war effort. They felt guilty that their friends remained in Spanish jails. As a result, the vacation went poorly.

Orwell returned home extremely anxious to write articles explaining the problems with the Communist Party in Spain. The *New Statesman* agreed to publish such an article, but when the editors saw it, they backed out because it would "cause trouble." Instead, they offered him the opportunity to review a book on the Spanish Civil War. Once he completed the review, the *New Statesman* would not print it on the grounds that, again, he had been too outspoken. In addition, Gollancz rejected his book proposal on the Spanish Civil War. All was not lost, however, for Orwell later published both the article and the review in other publications.

When the Orwells returned to Wallington, they found that Aunt Nellie had allowed the place to deteriorate. Instead of reopening the shop, they concentrated on getting their small farm up and running again.

Almost immediately Orwell began work on *Homage to Catalonia*, in which he wanted to capture the failure of the revolution in Spain. He completed a draft by early December and finished the book by mid-January 1938. Frederic Warburg would later publish the book.

During the past six years, Orwell had completed six books. His body was worn out from his bout with pneumonia in 1933 and his gunshot wound in 1937. Even so, he considered accepting a newspaper-editing job in India if both the Indian and British governments agreed. His health intervened, however. In March he developed a severe cough, which led to coughing up blood. He stayed at a sanatorium for a little over five months, where Eileen's brother worked as a doctor. Although his symptoms resembled tuberculosis, doctors could not confirm that he had the disease. They tried to keep him from writing as the effort exhausted him. Eileen traveled for visits every other week. Eventually Orwell was allowed to walk to the parish church and around its nearby graveyard. He also began jotting down ideas for *Coming Up For Air*, a humorous novel about a middle-aged insurance salesman who seeks escape into his childhood village but fails to recapture his childhood.

Meanwhile, reviews of *Homage to Catalonia* were favorable, but sales remained poor.

The doctors at the sanatorium suggested the Orwells travel someplace warmer and drier for the sake of George's health. They decided to go to the North African country of Morocco in September 1938, after accepting an anonymous loan from novelist L. H. Myers. Orwell was working on the manuscript that would become his novel *Coming Up for Air*. They lived in a villa outside Marrakech, where they kept a garden and a few farm animals. The paradoxical beauty and uncleanliness of the women and the poverty of the people intrigued Orwell.

In December both Orwells became ill because of bad drinking water. By January they felt better, and George had finished a draft of *Coming Up for Air*. At that point they took a vacation into nearby mountains, where they found the air refreshing.

After six months in Marrakech, Orwell and Eileen had had enough and wanted to return to England in March 1939. Orwell soon discovered that his father was dying of cancer. He returned to Southwold while Eileen went to visit her family. Eric helped his parents—doing housework, reading to his father, and telling stories about their stay in Marrakech. During his stay, both he and his mother had bouts with illness. He developed a high fever, and she had trouble with phlebitis. Eileen arrived to help while the two were ill. After about a week, Orwell felt better, and the couple returned to Wallington.

The Orwells traveled to Marrakech hoping the warm, dry weather would clear George's lungs. *(Courtesy of University College London.)*

In late April Orwell heard from Gollancz that he had reservations about publishing *Coming Up for Air*. In one section, a character gave an angry speech against the Left Book Club, Gollancz's own brainchild. Whereas before, Orwell had been willing to make necessary changes, now he was less willing. Gollancz went ahead with publishing anyway. The novel, to be the last book handled by Gollancz, was published in June 1939. In the next twelve years Orwell would write only three more novels.

This novel explored the life of insurance man George Bowling, who hid money from his wife so he could visit his childhood haunts. But he found that, as the present, the past changes as well. The places he went to were so different that it was not possible for him to rediscover his childhood.

In *Coming Up for Air*, Orwell again experimented with the inside/outside techniques he had learned from reading the works of James Joyce. Sometimes he used the viewpoint of the main character, George Bowling, and at other times he used that of himself.

Sales were better for this book than they had been with *Homage to Catalonia*. Three thousand copies sold, including 1000 as part of a second printing. Reviews were excellent.

At age eighty-two, on June 28, 1939, Mr. Blair died at home in Southwold. The death certificate stated "carcinoma of the intestines" as the cause. Orwell was with him when he died. He closed his father's eyes with the tradition of placing pennies on the eyelids. After the funeral, he did not know what to do with the pennies, so his friend Richard Rees threw them into the sea.

At the time that his father died, Orwell was working on a lengthy essay about the author Charles Dickens, whom he admired. The essay traces Dickens's faults—sentimentality, stereotyping, overgeneralizing the worlds of commercial and industrial work, clichéd endings, and a tendency to avoid tragedy. Orwell also revealed the writer's strengths. Dickens could portray the

Orwell admired Charles Dickens' ability to be "generously angry."
(Courtesy of The Library of Congress.)

common man with empathy and insight. He also believed in the freedom and equality of all people.

In a very real sense, Dickens was a moralist. That is, he wanted to improve the human condition through his writing. In discovering this side of Dickens, Orwell saw a parallel in himself. He imagined the face of Dickens was also his own:

> He is laughing, with a touch of anger in his laughter, but no triumph, no malignity. It is the face of a man who is always fighting against something, but who fights in the open and is not frightened, the face of a man who is *generously angry* . . . a type hated with equal hatred by all the smelly little orthodoxies which are now contending for our souls.

Both of his essays "Charles Dickens" and "Inside the Whale" come to the same conclusion: "Good novels are not written by orthodoxy-sniffers, nor by people who are conscience-stricken about their own orthodoxy. Good novels are written by people who are *not frightened.*"

George Orwell's greatest writing strengths appeared in his sketches, essays, reviews, and nonfiction books, but not in his novels. Unfortunately, he could not make as much money on the nonfiction forms as he could on the novels.

Three weeks before World War II began, two police detectives arrived at Orwell's home and confiscated some of his books that had been published by Obelisk

Press in Paris. Obelisk had a reputation for publishing obscene materials, including books by Henry Miller, whose work Orwell admired. The detectives took all Obelisk Press books. It shocked Orwell that censorship was occurring in England.

Chapter Eight

War Effort

Even though the censorship experience had left him bitter, Orwell tried to do his part in World War II. Writing was difficult because the war caused a shortage of both paper and publishers. Military authorities turned him down, perhaps because he was thirty-seven years old at the time, but also because of his lung condition and his wound from the Spanish Civil War. Ironically, Eileen obtained work in the Censorship Department in London. She commuted back to Wallington on weekends.

Hitler's army had conquered Norway by the end of April 1940. Soon afterwards, Hitler invaded the Netherlands. France would come under German control in June. The Orwells began hoarding potatoes in case of a food shortage. A friend described Orwell working in his garden at this time:

> He was standing with a hoe, looking very frail, deep-furrowed cheeks and pitifully feeble chest. His strong

cord trousers gave a massivity to his legs oddly in contrast to his emaciated torso. After tea we talked a great deal, he in that flat dead voice of his, never laughing beyond a sort of wistful chuckle, a weariness in all he said.

Eventually Orwell grew lonely for Eileen and moved to London. Their fourth-floor apartment, in a building with no elevator, had only two rooms. The furniture was second-hand, and they had to share a bathroom with other tenants.

Now that he was back in London, Orwell could start reviewing again. He wrote theater and book reviews for *Time and Tide* and *Tribune*. He now wrote reviews using a typewriter without drafts or revisions. Orwell's new writing method was faster and served to make his style more direct.

Eileen had always been very close to her brother, Laurence. When the war started, he volunteered to tend the wounded on the front. As a lung specialist, he was interested in learning more about chest wounds. Word came that he had been killed in the line of duty, hit by shrapnel hours before he was due to return home. Had he lived and continued his research, Laurence O'Shaughnessy might have been able to save Orwell when he was finally diagnosed with tuberculosis in 1947.

Her brother's death deeply disturbed Eileen. She once described their relationship to a friend: "If we were at opposite ends of the world and I sent him a telegram saying 'Come at once' he would have come, George would not do that. For him his work comes before anybody." She became very depressed.

Orwell persistently tried to enlist but without success. He also had trouble getting other work. He expanded his journalism by writing for Cyril Connolly's *Horizon*, and beginning in 1941 he wrote a column called "London Letter" for *Partisan Review* in New York. Cyril Connolly recalled what he was like at this time: "He reduced everything to politics . . . in fact it was an obsession. He could not blow his nose without moralising on conditions in the handkerchief industry . . . He felt enormously at home in the Blitz, among the bombs, the bravery, the rubble, the shortages, the homeless, the signs of rising revolutionary temper."

Orwell became increasingly well known as a journalist and as a writer in general. His friend Inez Holden recalled in her diary: "It's strange the way a writer's fame begins slowly creeping up on him and then racing . . . People of taste and sensitiveness, writers, political workers and actors . . . socialist doctors, factory workers, and technical instructors in touch with their labor organizations are all well aware of Orwell."

As Hitler's march seemed destined to trample England, Orwell joined the militia, known as the Home Guard. He also experimented with explosives, much as he had in his younger days. At one point, Eileen remarked, "I can put up with bombs on the mantelpiece, but I will not have a machine gun under the bed." Fredric Warburg, the publisher of *Homage to Catalonia*, reversed civilian roles by serving under Orwell in the Home Guard. He described what it was like: "As Sergeant Blair fell in as company marker for my first parade, I discerned the zeal which inflamed his tall skinny body. His uniform was crumpled, but it had been cut to fit him by a good tailor. The tricorn cap, bearing the badge of the King's Royal Rifle Corps . . . was perched so jauntily on the side of his head that I feared it might fall off."

The Blitz occurred in August, an attack on Britain which involved nightly bombing. The activity seemed to excite Orwell. After one raid he saw mannequins strewn on the pavement outside a department store, resembling dead human bodies. The scene reminded him of a similar experience in Spain, where plaster saints from churches had been thrown into the streets by the force of the bombing.

In 1941 Orwell published *The Lion and the Unicorn*. This book was one of several works by various authors designed to combat Nazism. With 12,000 copies sold, it became Orwell's biggest seller to date except for *The Road to Wigan Pier*. The work put his name in the forefront of those advocating socialistic reform. Invited to speak at a combined May meeting of the Oxford University English Club and the Democratic Social Club, he chose as his topic "Literature and Totalitarianism."

Out of all this celebrity came at last an opportunity for Orwell to serve in the war effort— as talks assistant at the Indian Office of the British Broadcasting Corporation (BBC). The radio talks, beamed to an Indian audience, served as propaganda to keep Indians loyal to Great Britain during the war.

Several problems with the job became apparent to Orwell fairly early. First, he was working in a large office as part of a huge bureaucratic organization, which was not his favorite kind of work. Second, problems with government censorship frequently arose. After a while he felt like "an orange that's been trodden on by a very dirty boot."

Orwell finally decided to leave the BBC when a survey revealed that his broadcasts were having little, if any, effect. Few Indians listened to the broadcasts, so they were useless. Moreover, the broadcast preparations took energy away from his other literary efforts.

A diary entry from the period states, "I am doing nothing that is not futility and have less and less to show for the time I waste . . . doing imbecile things . . . which in fact *don't* help . . . the war effort, but are considered necessary by the huge bureaucratic machine." Orwell left the BBC in September 1943.

Cyril Connolly introduced Orwell to David Astor at the *Observer*. Astor asked him to write articles and reviews for his publication. Originally Orwell planned to visit Africa and Italy as a war correspondent for the *Observer*, but his health would not allow such travel.

Just as he was leaving the BBC, the left-wing weekly *Tribune* asked him to serve as its literary editor. He accepted and stayed in that capacity for fifteen months, also writing a regular column called "As I Please." He himself admitted that editing was not his best talent. He made decisions slowly and, being a writer himself, tended to be too softhearted toward contributors. Years after his editorship had ended, he wrote, "[The *Tribune*] is the only existing weekly paper that makes a genuine effort to be both progressive and humane—that is, to combine a radical Socialist policy with a respect for freedom of speech and a civilised attitude towards literature and the arts."

Not long after the death of Eileen's brother, her mother died in 1941, and Eileen's depression worsened. While Orwell was working for the India office of the BBC, she worked at the Ministry of Food, supervising broadcasts of "The Kitchen Front." This program was designed to educate citizens in food preparation that followed the restrictions of wartime rationing.

The couple moved from an apartment to the lower half of a Victorian home. Orwell did some woodworking in the basement and illegally kept some chickens in the backyard. He once advised a friend: "It's not a good idea to give the chickens names because then you can't eat them." He said to another: "Don't you ever feel the need to do something with your hands? I'm surprised you don't . . . I've installed a lathe in the basement. I don't think I could exist without my lathe."

Orwell became more socially active. He often ate lunch with friends and stopped with them at a pub on the way home from work. His mother Ida and sister Avril also worked in London—Avril in a sheet-metal factory, Ida, now in her sixties, as a shop assistant in a department store. But in March 1943, Ida had difficulty breathing. She was taken to the hospital and one week later died of heart failure. Stress due to acute bronchitis and emphysema had probably brought on the heart failure .

After his mother's death, Orwell began to want a child. He had long asserted to many friends and to Eileen that he was sterile, although there is no medical evidence of this condition. When Orwell first raised the possibility of adoption with Eileen, she held back, wondering if she really wanted or could raise a child. They arranged an adoption through Gwen O'Shaughnessy, Eileen's sister-in-law and widow of brother Laurence. In June 1943, the couple welcomed baby Richard into their home. Eileen quickly became devoted to the child, and the couple drew closer than any time since their first year of marriage. Eventually she left her job with the Ministry of Food to care for Richard.

Orwell had finished the manuscript for *Animal Farm* two months before Richard was born. This little book would make him famous abroad as well as in England. The concepts behind *Animal Farm* had been germinating since his return from Spain. The book was an animal fable with strong parallels to contemporary politics.

Animal Farm is a political satire designed to destroy the public's belief in the myth about the Russian Revolution. The story is so well written that it can stand alone without extended references into political life. But a sophisticated reader can appreciate the broader tragedy of the animals' unsuccessful struggle against dictatorship. The farm animals, who represent the citizens, successfully rise up against Farmer Jones, who represents the Czarist regime. But they have difficulty maintaining their new society and soon submit to another tyrant, this time from among their own kind.

Animal Farm was an attack on Soviet Communism. At that time, Stalin, the leader of the Union of Soviet Socialist Republics (U.S.S.R.), was popular with the British public because his troops were fighting the Germans. Gollancz and other publishers approved of him. So as Orwell completed *Animal Farm*, many intellectuals were not examining the Soviet Union critically. Orwell knew he would have trouble getting sympathetic readers. In fact, Gollancz rejected the manuscript, as he felt that the book would bolster pro-Nazi propaganda. The manuscript met the same fate with three other firms.

The manuscript was nearly lost when Germany released V-1 bombs over London, and one hit the Orwell residence, causing the ceiling to fall in. Orwell found the typescript of *Animal Farm* in the wreckage and retrieved it, somewhat wrinkled. Then he sent it to his publisher Fredric Warburg, who accepted it. Warburg would very astutely hold up publication until after Hitler's defeat, when Stalin's popularity in England had lessened considerably.

During this time, Orwell stayed very busy. He worked as literary editor of *Tribune*, which included writing his regular column "As I Please." He continued to write his "London Letters" column for *Partisan Review* in America. He also wrote reviews for the *Observer* and the *Manchester Evening News*. On top of all this, he jumped at the opportunity to serve as a war correspondent for the *Observer* in France, and in February 1945 he left for Paris.

When he found that the famous American novelist Ernest Hemingway was staying at his hotel, he knocked at the author's room door. Hemingway was packing his bags, preparing to leave. At first, Orwell introduced himself as Eric Blair. Hemingway answered, "Well what . . . do you want?" Then he quickly introduced himself as George Orwell. Hemingway responded, "Why . . . didn't you say so?" and offered him a drink.

While Orwell was in France, Eileen's doctor found tumors on her uterus that signaled the need for a hysterectomy. In a letter to Orwell dated March 21 and 23, she explained, "By the time you get home I'll be convalescent at last and you won't have the hospital nightmare you would so much dislike." She knew how much he dreaded hospitals and how he got sick just visiting them. On March 29 she wrote him from her hospital bed as she waited for the operation: "Dearest I'm just going to have the operation, already enema'd, injected . . . cleaned and packed up."

During the operation Eileen suffered an allergic reaction to the anesthetic, which led to a heart attack. She died on the operating table at age thirty-nine. Her sister-in-law, Gwen O'Shaughnessy, cabled Orwell the shocking news. Later he recalled, "No one had anticipated anything going wrong, and I did not even hear she was to have the operation till the last moment . . . it was a horrible shock." Doreen Kopp, Gwen's sister who had married Georges Kopp, agreed to look after Richard until Orwell returned.

Chapter Nine

Work and Retreat

Orwell could not stand staying home and facing his grief. So he did what he so often had done in the past—he worked. He returned to correspondence reporting, this time in Germany, where he observed the German ruins, fleeing refugees, and dead soldiers. He also wrote about his views on Britain's response to the war:

> If I had to say what had most struck me about the behaviour of the British people during the war, I should point to the *lack* of reaction of any kind. In the face of terrifying dangers and golden political opportunities, people just keep on keeping on, in a sort of twilight sleep in which they are conscious of nothing except the daily round of work, family life, darts at the pub, exercising the dog, mowing the lawn, bringing home the supper beer, etc etc . . . Never would I have prophesied that we could go through nearly six years of war without arriving at either Socialism or Fascism, and with our civil liberties almost intact. I don't know whether this semi-

anaesthesia in which the British people contrive to live is a sign of decadence . . . or whether on the other hand it is a kind of instinctive wisdom.

In July 1945, after returning to England, Orwell hired twenty-eight-year-old Susan Watson as a live-in assistant to look after Richard. One of her legs had been crippled by cerebral palsy. He made no mention of this during the interview, but one test of her qualifications was to have her help give Richard a bath.

Susan adapted very well to life in the Orwell household. Orwell's usual workday began at eight or nine o'clock a.m. He worked at his writing until lunch, took a second break for high tea, then worked straight through again until early the next morning. She got used to hearing his typewriter through her sleep.

Susan discovered other traits, as well. Orwell liked to make his own gunpowder from scratch. Once he requested that she dye all his shirts navy blue. He did not buy Richard toys but instead gave him carpentry tools to play with. Orwell had a preference for odd items. Susan's grandmother once knitted him a pair of socks, one mistakenly larger than the other. He preferred these to his other socks.

After her death, Eileen's presence was still felt in the house. Her clothes hung in the closet. Her jewels remained in the jewelry box. Susan's eight-year-old daughter, Sally, asked why Orwell kept them. He answered evasively, "I'm saving them for a rainy day." She asked what he would do with them on a rainy day. He considered her questions, then responded, "Why, I think I'll give them to you, Sally." That's exactly what he ended up doing.

Animal Farm came out in Britain in August 1945, just as the Cold War was beginning. It sold more than 25,000 hardcover copies over the next five years—ten times the normal selling record for his books. The American edition came out in 1946. In over four years the American firm sold 590,000 copies.

Many readers found Orwell's message pessimistic. He defended himself as a realistic optimist, asserting that "you can't have a revolution unless you make it for yourself; there is no such thing as a benevolent dictatorship." Compared with his previous books, this one had more humor. Some readers thought this could be a sign of Eileen's influence, and in fact he admitted that she did have input during the structuring of the book. She had read sections of the book at night while Orwell was writing it.

The success of *Animal Farm* increased Orwell's popularity as a journalist. He received regular invitations to write articles and reviews for four publications: the *Evening Star*, the *Manchester Evening News*, the *Observer*, and the *Tribune*. As he was writing about real-world events in his novels, he also commented on them in his essays. In one essay, "Politics and the English Language," he argued that the decay of the English language parallels the greater decay of society. It was possible to reverse this decay by speaking and writing clearly.

In the year after his wife's death, Orwell put out over 130 articles and reviews. In April 1946, he published "A Good Word for the Vicar of Bray," just sixteen days after he had cleared the cottage of Eileen's belongings. Though the article centered around death, guilt, and immortality, it never mentioned his wife directly. This unwillingness to share feelings with others was typical of Orwell.

In addition to writing, Orwell had to care for his son, Richard, with help from Susan. He also gave talks to various groups and wrote scripts for the BBC. Such a schedule was difficult to maintain. In April 1946 he complained, "Everyone keeps coming at me wanting me to lecture, to write commissioned booklets, to join this and that, etc.—you don't know how I pine to get free of it all." The grueling schedule wore him down until he searched for escape.

In 1944 David Astor had recommended he investigate a country retreat on the Scottish island of Jura, where a large farmhouse called Barnhill was available. One of Eileen's last letters mentioned leaving Wallington for this isolated place, but she had not been keen to make the change. The five-bedroom home meant more housecleaning. The place had no electricity and stood far from civilization. The nearest neighbor lived over a mile away, the road to the home dwindled to just a path; the nearest shop was twenty-five miles away, and a population of only 300 lived on the surrounding 160 square miles.

After Eileen's death, Orwell thought again about moving to Jura. He felt living in the country would be good for Richard. Susan Watson could come along to help. With no phone and mail delivery only twice a week, he was attracted to the distance from public life. But there was one other problem. At the same time that he sought isolation, he also sought a wife.

In a desperate attempt to find another partner, he contacted Anne Popham, who lived in his London apartment building. In a letter to her, he called himself "unattractive, unhealthy, and old," but he also pointed out that he was worth a considerable sum of money. He added: "What I am really asking you is whether you would like to be the widow of a literary man . . . You would probably get royalties coming in . . . You are young and healthy, and deserve somebody better than me: on the other hand . . . you might do worse." Anne rejected his proposal.

Next, he tried Celia Paget. His friend Arthur Koestler had introduced him to his sister-in-law earlier. She took more time than Anne to consider his proposal, but she too decided against marriage.

Celia had a friend named Sonia Brownell who worked with her at *Horizon* under Orwell's old friend Cyril Connolly. Sonia was Connolly's editorial assistant and had many responsibilities at the magazine. She had met Orwell in 1945 and thought him very cold and distant, but gradually she had become interested in him. Later she would praise him as "the only intellectual who could mend a fuse or an iron." He liked her unaffected, straightforward manner, and he realized that she could look out for his interests. Sometime between 1945 and 1946 he proposed to her, but nothing came of the offer. Between 1947 and 1949 they rarely saw each other.

Once Orwell, Richard, and Susan had moved to Jura in the summer of 1946, Orwell invited women friends to visit, but each one left after a brief stay. After all, it was an eight-mile walk from the road to the rustic, old house. In addition, they had the chance to observe Orwell's eccentricities, such as his insisting on making his own matches.

Susan's crippled leg proved a difficulty in the rugged terrain. Orwell's unmarried sister Avril, who had come to Barnhill that summer, began to take over Susan's chores. Soon domestic battles arose between the two women. Avril criticized Susan for working slowly. Orwell tried to distance himself from the battleground. He felt some loyalty to his sister because their sister, Marjorie, had died in May 1946 of a kidney ailment at age forty-eight. In seven years the family had lost father, mother, and sister.

Susan could stand the situation no longer and decided to leave. Avril stayed on until the end of Orwell's life and later, appreciating the rough life on Jura. A month after her arrival, she wrote:

> Eric has bought a little boat & we go fishing in the evening . . . when the fish rise. They are simply delicious fresh from the sea. In fact . . . we live on the fat of the land. Plenty of eggs & milk & ½ lb. butter

> extra each weekly on to our rations. Our landlord
> gave us a large hunk of venison a short while ago
> which was extremely good. Then there are local
> lobsters & crabs . . . I am really enjoying it all
> immensely.

In the autumn of 1946 the three returned to London
to stay for the next seven months. In August Orwell
began a new novel and became intent on trying to live
at Barnhill a full year. Jura offered a quietness that
Orwell felt helped him to write. Meanwhile, in London
he kept himself from becoming too busy again. He
worked only on his "As I Please" column for *Tribune.*

London's winter of 1946 was severe, with numerous
fuel shortages. When he ran out of coal, Orwell burned
peat. When he ran out of peat, he burned some old
furniture. As might be expected, the cold weather ag-
gravated his lung condition. Avril remembered, "We
had no fuel, and Eric had been ill on and off during the
winter . . . We even got to the point of chopping up
young Richard's toys and putting them on the fire in
Eric's room to try and keep him warm while he was
writing." In the spring of 1947, Orwell, Richard, and
Avril returned to Jura. Orwell was still struggling with
his lung condition and working on his new novel.

Orwell had a close call while boating with relatives
during the summer of 1947. He was returning from a
trip to the other side of the island with Avril, Richard,
and Marjorie's three children who were visiting on vacation. Orwell steered the boat into a treacherous gulf

where whirlpools threatened to suck the craft down. He later wrote to Brenda Salkeld:

> Four of us including Richard were nearly drowned. We got into the pool, owing to trying to go through the gulf at the wrong state of the tide, and the outboard motor was sucked off the boat. We managed to get out of it with the oars and then got to one of the little islands . . . The sea was pretty bad and the boat turned over as we were going ashore, so that we lost everything we had including the oars and . . .12 blankets.

Orwell completed the first draft of his new novel, *Nineteen Eighty-four,* on Jura toward the end of 1947. *Nineteen Eighty-four* was an anti-utopian novel. He described it as "a fantasy . . . in the form of a naturalistic novel." Orwell inverted the upcoming year 1948 to the Nineteen Eighty-four of the future. The novel follows the protagonist, Winston, in his questioning of the new social order and his pursuit of love—an emotion that is now forbidden. His girlfriend, Julia, is able to provide Winston with clues about the totalitarian regime.

The message of *Nineteen Eighty-four* was a prophecy, warning of dire consequences in the future if people become complacent about government. Orwell explained:

> I do not believe that the kind of society I describe necessarily *will* arrive, but I believe . . . that some-

thing resembling it could arrive . . . The scene of the book is laid in Britain in order to emphasize that the English-speaking races are not innately better than anyone else and that totalitarianism, *if not fought against*, could triumph anywhere.

In *Nineteen Eighty-four*, Orwell realized his goal to make political writing into an art.

Chapter Ten

Immortality

In November 1947 Orwell had a bad coughing spell. When he spit up blood, he was taken to a hospital just outside Glasgow, Scotland. Here, doctors finally diagnosed his illness as tuberculosis. A new drug was now available called streptomycin. David Astor volunteered to pay anonymously for the expensive treatment. However, when doctors gave Orwell the drug, the dosages were too strong, causing his skin to turn red and his hair to fall out. His lungs, however, did clear. He stayed in the hospital until July 1948.

Back home on Jura that summer, he resumed the same driving pace. By November 1948 he had finished revising *Nineteen Eighty-four*, but it needed retyping. Barnhill was so far from civilization that Orwell could not get a typist to make the trip, so he undertook the work himself, even though his bad health was returning. After three weeks, he sent the manuscript to London early in December.

By this time he was coughing up blood again. Gwen O'Shaughnessy arranged for Orwell to stay in a sanatorium, which he left for in early 1949 accompanied by Richard Rees. The doctors gave him another new drug, para-amino-salicylic acid (PAS), which made him feel constantly nauseated. When doctors switched him back to streptomycin, the results were worse than before. His lungs did not clear as well, and the reddening of his skin and hair loss increased.

During Orwell's first month at the sanatorium, his publisher Fredric Warburg visited with good news: He liked *Nineteen Eighty-four*. He planned to have the galley proofs ready by March and the book ready by June. Orwell's agent, Leonard Moore, had arranged for Harcourt Brace to be the American publisher. The novel met the public in June with rave reviews. Its realism ensured that it would reach beyond propaganda and would speak meaningfully to later generations.

Sonia Brownell visited Orwell at the sanatorium. Recovering from a failed love affair, she wanted to see how he was and offer her help. Orwell proposed again, and she promised to consider the possibility. *Horizon*, where she worked, might close its doors soon. She knew that with Orwell she would have both a cause to work for and financial stability. In turn, Orwell hoped that marrying Sonia might bolster him and giving him a reason to regain his health. By July she had agreed to marry him.

In September Orwell was moved to London College Hospital, where he would be nearer to Sonia. She bought an expensive engagement ring. The two married in his hospital room on October 13, 1949. David Astor was the best man. Orwell seemed genuinely happy. During the next three months Sonia visited him daily and handled his business affairs.

But by the end of 1949, his health had grown steadily worse. The couple planned to move to a Swiss sanatorium toward the end of January 1950. About a week before the scheduled departure, Sonia was at a nightclub with a friend when she received a call from the hospital. Shortly after midnight on January 21, 1950, Orwell's lungs had given out and he had died. He was forty-six years old.

To understand Orwell's legacy, he must be seen for the critic of falsehoods that he was. In one of his essays he stated:

> A known fact may be so unbearable that it is habitually pushed aside and not allowed to enter into logical processes, or on the other hand it may enter into every calculation and yet never be admitted as a fact, even in one's own mind . . . In 1927 Chiang Kai Shek boiled hundreds of communists alive, and yet within ten years he had become one of the heroes of the Left. The realignment of world politics had brought him into the anti-fascist camp and so it was felt that the boiling of the Communists didn t count, or perhaps had not happened.

Orwell was obsessed with the roles of the individual and the state. His reverence for freedom, justice, and mutual respect is still relevant today.

Orwell wished to be buried by the rites of the Church of England. The day of the funeral, January 25, 1950, was cold, and the church was unheated. He was buried in a country churchyard. The inscription on his headstone read:

HERE LIES
ERIC ARTHUR BLAIR
BORN JUNE 25TH 1903
DIED JANUARY 21ST 1950

Orwell left a large insurance policy to his son, Richard. Everything else went to Sonia. Sonia gave over care of Richard, now five years old, to Avril. In 1960, with Orwell's friends, David Astor and Richard Rees, Sonia established the George Orwell Archive at the Library of University College London. She also co-edited a four-volume collection of his essays, journalism, and letters. In the 1970s it became clear that she was an alcoholic, and she developed cancer. She died on December 11, 1980, at age sixty-two.

After Sonia's death, the Orwell estate went to Richard, who was then in his thirties. He was working for a company that made farm machinery. He used the name Richard Blair and remained away from the public eye. The only document he saved was his adoption certificate, with the names of his birth parents intentionally burned away by one of Orwell's cigarettes.

Works by George Orwell

Glossary

academics: school studies or course work.

admonish: give friendly earnest advice; warn.

Anarchist: one who believes that government is unnecessary and prefers voluntary cooperation.

anonymity: the quality or state of not being named or identified.

blitz: intensive aerial bombing campaign.

bronchitis: inflammation of the bronchial tubes.

cliche: marked by trite phrases, expressions, or beliefs.

Communist: one who adheres to the doctrine based on revolutionary Marxian socialism and Marxism-Leninism that was the official ideology of the USSR.

convalescent: relating to recovery from injury or illness.

debris: remains of something broken down or destroyed.

delta: alluvial deposit at the mouth of a river.

detrimental: harmful.

domination: exercise of controlling influence.

empathy: being sensitive to the feelings of another.

emphysema: abnormal dilation of lung's air spaces and distension of its walls.

Fascist: movement that exalts nationalism and often race above the individual. A Fascist state has a centralized autocratic government headed by a dictatorial leader.

fragmentary: having fragments; incomplete.

galley proof: a final proof of a manuscript before publication.

hop: a plant used to make beer.

hysterectomy: surgical removal of the uterus.

imperialism: policy of extending the power of a nation over other nations.

inequity: injustice or unfairness.

infer: to make a guess based on information at hand.

libel: statement or representation that conveys an unjustly negative impression.

literary: of or relating to books or writing.

malignity: evil intent.

massivity: bulk or largeness.

moralist: one concerned with regulating the morals of others.

Nazi: member of German Nazi party under Hitler from 1933 to 1945.

nostalgia: longing for a return to the past.

obscenity: quality or state of inciting lust or depravity.

orthodoxy: quality or state of following the standard in religion or, sometimes, politics.

parapet: wall.

phlebitis: inflammation of a vein.

prestigious: best known through positive reputation.

propriety: quality or state of being proper; conformity to what is socially acceptable.

provincialism: a manner of speech or accent typical of a certain region; having a narrow or restricted outlook

public school: in Britain, a private school that prepares students for the university

rectory: residence of parish priest.

sanatorium: a retreat that provides therapy combined with rest, diet, and exercise for treatment or rehabilitation.

scullion: kitchen helper.

Socialist: one who believes in collective or government ownership and administration of the means to produce and distribute the goods of a nation.

socio-economic: class based on place in society and earning power.

stereotype: an oversimplified opinion, usually of a person or group.

teak: wood from an Indian timber tree used for furniture and shipbuilding.

tuberculosis: a disease characterized by a primary infection in the lungs, fever, and spitting of blood.

verisimilitude: the quality or state of appearing true or depicting realism.

Bibliography

Crick, Bernard. *George Orwell: A Life*. Boston: Little, Brown, 1980.

Kalechofsky, Roberta. *George Orwell*. Modern Literature Monographs. New York: Frederick Ungar, 1973.

Orwell, George. *Collected Essays, Journalism, and Letters of George Orwell*. 4 vols. ed. Sonia Orwell and Ian Angus. New York: Harcourt, Brace & World, 1968.

Orwell, George. *The Orwell Reader*. New York: Harcourt, Brace, 1956.

Rees, Richard. *George Orwell: Fugitive from the Camp of Victory*. Carbondale, IL: Southern Illinois UP, 1962.

Shelden, Michael. *Orwell: The Authorized Biography*. New York: HarperCollins, 1991.

Stansky, Peter, and William Abrahams. *Orwell: The Transformation*. London: Granada, 1981.

———. *The Unknown Orwell*. New York: Alfred A. Knopf, 1972.

Woodcock, George. *The Crystal Spirit: A Study of George Orwell*. Boston: Little, Brown, 1966.

Wykes, David. *A Preface to Orwell*. Preface Books. London: Longman, 1987.

Sources

CHAPTER ONE—Childhood Pain and Joy

p. 9, "Here is a little . . ." George Orwell, "Such, Such Were the Joys," 1952, *The Orwell Reader* (New York: Harcourt, Brace, 1956), 420.

p. 10, "Report yourself . . ." Ibid., 421.

p. 10, "Look what . . ." Ibid., 422.

p. 12, "I had the lonely . . ." George Orwell, "Why I Write," 1947, *The Orwell Reader* (New York: Harcourt, Brace, 1956), 390.

p. 15, "Perhaps the greatest . . ." Michael Shelden, *Orwell: The Authorized Biography* (New York: HarperCollins, 1991), 37.

p. 15, "Do you think . . ." Ibid., 38.

p. 16, "I can still remember . . ." Ibid., 46.

p. 18, "Do come before . . ." Ibid., 47.

p. 18, "You are noticed . . ." Crick, Bernard, *George Orwell: A Life*. (Boston: Little, Brown, 1980), 39.

CHAPTER TWO—Sidestepping the University

p. 21, "You're wanted . . ." Shelden, *Authorized Biography*, 61.

p. 21, "Once he was . . ." Crick, *A Life*, 51.

p. 22, "To be as slack . . ." Shelden, *Authorized Biography*, 64.

p. 22, "never had a . . ." Ibid., 67.

p. 23, "The feature of . . ." Crick, *A Life*, 68-69.

p. 26, "To serve . . ." Peter Stansky and William Abrahams, *The Unknown Orwell* (New York: Alfred A. Knopf, 1972), 151.

p. 28, "pagodas, pariahs . . ." Shelden, *Authorized Biography*, 90.

p. 30, "The banana is . . ." Ibid., 90.

p. 30, ". . . he had goats . . ." Ibid., 102.

p. 31, "loneliness, boredom . . ." Stansky and Abrahams, *Unknown Orwell*, 192.

p. 31, "did not seem . . ." Ibid., 194.

p. 32, "In Moulmein . . ." George Orwell, "Shooting an Elephant," 1936, *The Orwell Reader* (New York: Harcourt, Brace, 1956), 3.

p. 32, "haunted by . . ." Shelden, *Authorized Biography*, 106.

p. 32, "Give an inch . . ." Ibid., 107.

p. 32, "Unfortunately . . ." Ibid., 111.

CHAPTER THREE—Struggling Writer

p. 33, "his father was . . ." Shelden, *Authorized Biography*, 115.

p. 34, "In the Indian . . ." Ibid., 116.

p. 34, "awkward and contrived" Stansky and Abrahams, *Unknown Orwell*, 225.

p. 35, ". . . whether he . . ." Richard Rees, *George Orwell: Fugitive from the Camp of Victory*, Crosscurrents/Modern Critiques (Carbondale, IL: Southern Illinois UP, 1962), 119.

p. 36, "I had never..." Orwell, "How the Poor Die," 1950, *The Orwell Reader* (New York: Harcourt, Brace, 1956), 87.

p. 39, "too short . . ." Crick, *A Life*, 132.

CHAPTER FOUR—Reluctant Teacher

p. 42, "The miserable . . ." George Orwell, letter to Leonard Moore, 23 Dec. 1932, *Collected Essays, Journalism, and Letters of George Orwell*, ed. Sonia Orwell and Ian Angus, vol. 1 (New York: Harcourt, Brace & World, 1968), 110.

p. 44, "I do know that . . ." George Orwell, letter to the Editor of *The Times*, 11 Feb. 1933, *Collected Essays, Journalism, and Letters of George Orwell*, ed. Sonia Orwell and Ian Angus, vol. 1 (New York: Harcourt, Brace & World, 1968), 224.

p. 45, "I wanted to write..." Orwell, "Why I Write," 1947, *The Orwell Reader* (New York: Harcourt, Brace, 1956), 391.

p. 48, "I am not..." George Woodcock, *The Crystal Spirit: A Study of George Orwell* (Boston: Little, Brown, 1966), 126.

CHAPTER FIVE—The Making of a Socialist

p. 51, "a tall, big-headed..." Shelden, *Authorized Biography*, 204.

p. 52, "I don't know . . ." Ibid., 209.

p. 52, "Mr. Orwell . . ." Ibid., 254.

p. 54, "Through my . . ." Ibid., 214.

p. 55, "What I have most . . ." Orwell, "Why I Write," 394.

p. 58, The writer of..." Shelden, *Authorized Biography*, 238.

p. 58, "a silly . . ." Ibid., 239.

CHAPTER SIX—Marriage and War

p. 59, "I'm afraid I . . ." George Orwell, letter to Denys King-Farlow, 9 June 1936, *Collected Essays, Journalism, and Letters of George Orwell*, ed. Sonia Orwell and Ian Angus, vol. 1 (New York: Harcourt, Brace & World, 1968), 116.

p. 63, "make political . . ." Orwell, "Why I Write," 394.

p. 64, "Blair is a fine . . ." Shelden, *Authorized Biography*, 256.

p. 64, "was afraid . . ." Ibid., 260.

p. 66, "Orwell stood up . . ." Ibid., 260.

p. 66, "He arrived . . ." Ibid., 263.

p. 66, "could not join . . ." Ibid., 266-267.

CHAPTER SEVEN—Illness Haunts

p. 68, "cause trouble" Shelden, *Authorized Biography*, 277.

p. 72, "carcinoma of the . . ." Ibid., 312.

p. 74, "He is laughing . . ." Ibid., 315.

p. 74, "Good novels . . ." George Orwell, "Inside the Whale," 1940, *Collected Essays* (London: Mercury, 1966), 159.

CHAPTER EIGHT—War Effort

p. 76, "He was standing . . ." Shelden, *Authorized Biography,* 322.

p. 77, "If we . . ." Crick, *A Life*, 264.

p. 78, "He reduced . . ." Ibid., 266.

p 78, "It's strange . . ." Ibid., 267-268.

p. 78, "I can put . . ." Shelden, *Authorized Biography*, 326.

p. 79, "As Sergeant Blair . . ." Ibid., 328.

p. 80, "an orange . . ." Orwell, letter to Rayner Heppenstall, 24 Aug. 1943, *Collected Essays, Journalism, and Letters of George Orwell*, ed. Sonia Orwell and Ian Angus, vol. 2 (New York: Harcourt, Brace & World, 1968), 305.

p. 80, "I am doing . . ." Shelden, *Authorized Biography*, 347-348.

p. 81 ". . . [The *Tribune*] is the . . ." George Orwell, "As I Pleased," 31 Jan. 1947, *Collected Essays, Journalism, and Letters of George Orwell*, ed. Sonia Orwell and Ian Angus, vol. 4 (New York: Harcourt, Brace & World, 1968), 280.

p. 81, "It's not a good . . ." Shelden, *Authorized Biography,* 359.

p. 81, "Don't you ever . . ." Ibid., 361.

p. 84, "Well what . . ." Ibid., 376.

p. 84, "By the time . . ." Ibid., 379.

p. 85, "Dearest . . ." Ibid., 380.

p. 85, "No one had . . ." Ibid., 381.

CHAPTER NINE—Work and Retreat

p. 86, ". . . if I had to . . ." George Orwell, "London Letter," 5 June 1945, *Collected Essays, Journalism, and Letters of George Orwell*, ed. Sonia Orwell and Ian Angus, vol. 3 (New York: Harcourt, Brace & World, 1968), 384-385.

p. 87, "I'm saving . . ." Shelden, *Authorized Biography,* 388.

p. 88, "you can't . . ." Ibid., 371.

p. 89, "Everyone keeps . . ." Orwell, letter to Arthur Koestler, 13 Apr. 1946, *Collected Essays, Journalism, and Letters of George Orwell*, ed. Sonia Orwell and Ian Angus, vol. 4 (New York: Harcourt, Brace & World, 1968), 146.

p. 90, "unattractive . . ." Shelden, *Authorized Biography*, 404.

p. 90, "the only . . ." Ibid., 407.

p. 91, ". . . Eric has bought . . ." Ibid., 415.

p. 92, "We had no . . ." Ibid., 418.

p. 93, "Four of us . . ." Ibid., 423.

p. 93, "a fantasy" David Wykes, *A Preface to Orwell,* Preface Books (London: Longman, 1987), 134.

p. 93, "I do not . . ." Ibid., 145-146.

CHAPTER TEN—Immortality

p. 97, "A known fact . . ." Rees, *Fugitive From the Camp,* 114-115.

Index